# A Life Coach Jou
## My Song-

## Self-Guided Life Coaching

Over your lifetime, as you grow and change, this Life Coaching Journal can be used over and over by using notebooks to write your journaling responses.

**Martie Morris Lee**

This book is dedicated to all the courageous teens I have had the pleasure of being associated with who have stepped up to do the hard work of discovering and working towards a life that is full of positive possibilities and options.

# My Song –

## A Life Coaching Journal for Teen Girls

My Song – is a life coaching journal that will guide you in composing your life-song. You will design, re-launch and unleash your dreams, your goals, and your potential... and you will sing your new song.

The life-coaching exercises, together with visualization and affirmations work together to provide a sound structure for you to compose and then begin the process of living your life-song.

The journal also includes opportunities to open journal about whatever is in your heart.

The author, Martie Morris Lee is a certified life coach and with this journal, she shares her brand of life coaching and her passion for optimism, growth and healing. The journaling prompts that serve as your life coach are the same prompts that she uses to empower women and teens in her life coaching services.

Prior to becoming a certified life coach, Martie spent 20 years as an executive director of a non-profit that is in the business of empowering women, teens and children and she developed several youth personal development programs.

# Your Guided Journey Will Guide You To
# Compose Your Life-Song

| Page | Topic |
|------|-------|
| 7 | Who Am I |
| 11 | Born To |
| 17 | Positive People |
| 18 | Super Special |
| 20 | Fake? |
| 21 | Masks |
| 24 | Longing to Belong |
| 28 | BFF & BFFs |
| 33 | Sister-hood or Clique? |
| 40 | Power of Words |
| 51 | Response To Mean Girls |
| 52 | Drama Queen or Communication Reaction |
| 55 | Negative Free |
| 58 | Kindness |
| 61 | Cyber Bullying |
| 63 | Life Roles |
| 65 | Leadership |
| 69 | Purpose |
| 72 | Body Image |
| 75 | Real Women-Real Teens |
| 79 | Tips for Healthy Body Image |
| 81 | Loneliness |
| 83 | Risks |
| 85 | Fear |
| 89 | Self-Harming Behaviors     92 Self Soothing |
| 94 | Letting Grudges Go |
| 104 | Vision |
| 108 | Design or Redesign Personal Brand |
| 125-158 | Life Coaching Gauge, Aspirations, Goals, Roadblocks, Limiting beliefs, Realistic Action Plans |
| 159 | Life Coaching Inspirational Journaling |

### Journaling Tips for the Life Coaching and
### Open Journaling Pages that Come from Your Heart.

- Be Consistent. Make journaling a habit by working towards a specific time of day that fits your schedule-possibly before going to bed, before breakfast, or after dinner.

- Don't edit or worry about grammar or spelling.

- Write any way you want... upside down... sideways...

- Be totally honest in your thinking and in your writing. Don't let fear stop you from deep inner reflection or from writing.

- Write about your thoughts and feelings – not just your day's activities.

- Don't just write about the things that went wrong but also focus on the positive aspects of your day and your life even if they are simple things.

- Concentrating on the positive will help you move towards your goals.

- Developing habits of positive thinking and writing will help you to become brave in the sense that no matter what happens in your life, you will be able to face it optimistically.

- You are on a journey and some days you will have much to write and other days it might be difficult to express your thoughts.

### Let the writing of your life-song begin!!!!

This Journal Belongs To

_____

Date _____

Location _____

## My Song -   Who Am I? Verse 1

"If you cannot teach me to fly, teach me to sing."
— J.M. Barrie, Peter Pan

The next few pages are a warm-up to help you start thinking about yourself.  It also gives you a framework for when you come back, maybe years later, and re-read your very first journal entries.  Write the first thing that comes to mind.

My name is _____

My nickname _____

I live with _____

My very favorite food is _____

I'm in grade_____

My favorite subject in school is _____

My all-time favorite teacher is _____

My favorite after school activity is _____

On weekends I like to _____

My favorite music _____

Three words that I use to describe me are

_____

Three words that describe my friends are

_____

# Verse 2

Three words that my parents use to describe me

_____

Three words my teachers would use to describe me

_____

One friend I can really talk to is _____

Some adults I can talk to are _____

My greatest strengths are

_____

Do you want to continue go on to college or a technical school?

_____

Do you participate in athletics, band or other after-school activities?

_____

What do you stand for?

_____
_____
_____
_____
_____
_____
_____
_____
_____
_____
_____
_____
_____
_____
_____

## The thing(s) I wish other people would get about me...

_____
_____
_____
_____
_____
_____
_____
_____
_____
_____
_____
_____
_____
_____
_____
_____
_____
_____
_____
_____
_____
_____
_____
_____
_____
_____
_____
_____
_____
_____
_____
_____
_____
_____

## With all my heart...I wish ...

## I Was Born To.....

*"Believe with all your heart that you will do what you were made to do."*
— Orison Swett Marden

**It may change, but at this point in my life, I feel I was absolutely born to...**

_____

_____

_____

_____

_____

_____

_____

_____

_____

_____

_____

_____

_____

_____

_____

_____

_____

_____

_____

_____

_____

_____

_____

_____

_____

# Life Coaching

"Music is an outburst of the soul." — Frederick Delius

Open journal about whatever is in your heart today.
Remember to include the positive!

_____
_____
_____
_____
_____
_____
_____
_____
_____
_____
_____
_____
_____
_____
_____
_____
_____
_____
_____
_____
_____
_____
_____
_____
_____
_____
_____
_____
_____
_____
_____
_____
_____

## *My Life Journey-Childhood*

*God gave us memory that we might have roses in December.*
—Sir James Barrie

Journal about positive things you remember from your childhood ages
1 to now. What are your favorite memories?

_____

_____

_____

_____

_____

_____

_____

_____

_____

_____

_____

_____

_____

_____

_____

_____

_____

_____

_____

_____

_____

_____

_____

_____

_____

_____

_____

_____

_____

_____

## Life Coaching

"Music gives a soul to the universe, wings to the mind, flight to the imagination and life to everything." — Plato

Open journal about whatever is in your heart today.
Remember to include the positive!

_____
_____
_____
_____
_____
_____
_____
_____
_____
_____
_____
_____
_____
_____
_____
_____
_____
_____
_____
_____
_____
_____
_____
_____
_____
_____
_____
_____
_____
_____
_____

*"Look at that sea, girls--all silver and shadow and vision of things not seen. We couldn't enjoy its loveliness any more if we had millions of dollars and ropes of diamonds."* — L.M. Montgomery, *Anne of Green Gables*

If you won the lottery and money was not an issue... how would you spend your time in several areas of your life?  Spiritual, emotional, family & friend relationships, school, wellness, leisure.

_____
_____
_____
_____
_____
_____
_____
_____
_____
_____
_____
_____
_____
_____
_____
_____
_____
_____
_____
_____
_____
_____
_____
_____
_____
_____
_____
_____
_____
_____

## Life Coaching

Open journal about whatever is in your heart today.
Remember to include the positive!

## Positive People

This list is typical of the responses when asking people what characteristics they see in positive people.

refuse to listen to gossip
are optimistic
believe the best of others
build others up
are happy on the inside
look for the good in things & people
talk about the good in things & people

say why they like things and people, not why they don't
look for opportunity when something bad happens
forgive people
if they have nothing nice to say, they say nothing
use positive language
avoid can't & won't
have a positive self-image
work to build their positive attitude
help others without expectation or measuring
help people
encourage others to succeed
are happy about themselves and their life
work on their attitude
ignore people who try to discourage them or tell them 'you can't'
count their blessings
believe in themselves & others
encourage themselves & others

**Add additional characteristics about positive people.**

_____
_____
_____
_____
_____
_____

## Super-Special

*There are powers inside of you which, if you could discover and use, would make of you everything you ever dreamed or imagined you could become.*
-Orison Swett Marden

Is it easy to point out your flaws to other people?
Is it difficult to point out your good points to others?

Journal about your self-worth, your confidence and your attributes that are super-special.

_____
_____
_____
_____
_____
_____
_____
_____
_____
_____
_____
_____
_____
_____
_____
_____
_____
_____
_____
_____
_____
_____
_____
_____
_____
_____
_____
_____
_____

# Life Coaching

"Music is the universal language of mankind."
— Henry Wadsworth Longfellow

Open journal about whatever is in your heart today.
Remember to include the positive!

_____
_____
_____
_____
_____
_____
_____
_____
_____
_____
_____
_____
_____
_____
_____
_____
_____
_____
_____
_____
_____
_____
_____
_____
_____
_____
_____
_____
_____

## *Fake?*

Does your personality ever change when you associate with different individuals or groups? Journal about why you think it changes. Do you ever feel like a 'fake'?  If so... journal about those experiences or journal about whatever this page has brought to your mind.

_____

_____

_____

_____

_____

_____

_____

_____

_____

_____

_____

_____

_____

_____

_____

_____

_____

_____

_____

_____

_____

_____

_____

_____

_____

_____

_____

_____

_____

_____

_____

_____

# Emotional Masks

Think about the masks that some people that you know wear. Maybe one wears a mask of being overly responsible to cover their fear of something that has happened to them.  Or maybe one wears a mask of silliness to cover self-doubt? Maybe one wears a mask of troublemaker to cover problems at home? Maybe one wears a mask to cover a hurting heart because someone has called them hurtful names or made fun of their weight?

Journal about the masks you might wear. Do you sometimes try to hide your true self at home to keep from getting in trouble? Do you sometimes wear a mask at school so that you fit in? What mask might you wear around boys? Around friends? Around teachers?

_____

_____

_____

_____

_____

_____

_____

_____

_____

_____

_____

_____

_____

_____

_____

_____

_____

_____

_____

_____

_____

_____

_____

## *Drop the Mask Anyone?*

There are many other behaviors that we can use as masks to cover our inner feelings. Some mask themselves by doing whatever it takes to make others happy. Some use a mask of anger to help avoid pain. Some use a happy-go-lucky mask.  Some tear others down. Some gossip. Some become the life of the party.
Some use alcohol or drugs to mask emotions.

From your previous list of masks, select one or two that you would like to get rid of in order to just be your true authentic self at all times.

Journal about how you might eliminate those masks.

_____

_____

_____

_____

_____

_____

_____

_____

_____

_____

_____

_____

_____

_____

_____

_____

_____

_____

_____

_____

_____

_____

_____

_____

# Life Coaching

Open journal about whatever is in your heart today.
Remember to include the positive!

_____
_____
_____
_____
_____
_____
_____
_____
_____
_____
_____
_____
_____
_____
_____
_____
_____
_____
_____
_____
_____
_____
_____
_____
_____
_____
_____
_____
_____
_____
_____
_____

## Longing To Belong

Belonging to a group of friends provides connections and that can be wonderful but it can also have problems such as the pressure to look or act in certain ways in order to maintain the connection. Sometimes girls are willing to do things that go against their beliefs or values... or they may do things that they really don't want to do in order to maintain their connection to the group.

**Journal your thoughts and feelings.**

_____
_____
_____
_____
_____
_____
_____
_____
_____
_____
_____
_____
_____
_____
_____
_____
_____
_____
_____
_____
_____
_____
_____
_____
_____
_____

**Journal about why do you think it's hard for some girls to say no to their friends?**

_____
_____
_____
_____
_____
_____
_____
_____
_____
_____

What are some things you would not do?

_____
_____
_____
_____
_____
_____
_____
_____
_____

Why do you think girls continue to be friends with people that ask them to do things that go against their beliefs or values?

_____
_____
_____
_____
_____
_____

## Journal your thoughts and feelings about what you think can be done to help girls have healthy friendships?

# Life Coaching

Open journal about whatever is in your heart today.
Remember to include the positive!

_____

_____

_____

_____

_____

_____

_____

_____

_____

_____

_____

_____

_____

_____

_____

_____

_____

_____

_____

_____

_____

_____

_____

_____

_____

_____

_____

_____

_____

_____

_____

_____

_____

_____

_____

_____

## Journal About Your Absolute # 1 BFF

Describe your relationship in detail. What do you do... what do you talk about... or laugh about... or cry about? What do you do when your friend is upset? Or tells you a secret?

_____
_____
_____
_____
_____
_____
_____
_____
_____
_____
_____
_____
_____
_____
_____
_____
_____

What does your friend do... when you are upset?
Or if you share a secret?

_____
_____
_____
_____
_____
_____
_____
_____
_____

**Journal About Your Group of BFFs**

Describe your group of BFFs in detail.
When do you hang out... what do you do... what do you talk about?
Laugh about? Where do you go?

_____

_____

_____

_____

_____

_____

_____

_____

_____

_____

_____

_____

_____

_____

_____

_____

_____

_____

_____

_____

_____

_____

_____

_____

_____

_____

_____

_____

_____

_____

## Life Coaching

"Where words fail, music speaks."  — Hans Christian Andersen

Open journal about whatever is in your heart today.
Remember to include the positive!

## *Journal Your Thoughts About the Following Characteristics*

• Trustworthy • Respectful • Caring • Honest • Tolerant • Respect for Actions & Decisions • Empathetic • Helpful • Pride in Self & Others • Cooperative • Compassionate • Understanding • Fair • Stand Up for Self Respectfully • Supportive • Kind

_____
_____
_____
_____
_____
_____
_____
_____
_____
_____
_____
_____
_____

Journal how you would describe a person or group with those characteristics.

_____
_____
_____
_____
_____
_____
_____
_____
_____
_____
_____

# Life Coaching

Open journal about whatever is in your heart today.
Remember to include the positive!

_____

_____

_____

_____

_____

_____

_____

_____

_____

_____

_____

_____

_____

_____

_____

_____

_____

_____

_____

_____

_____

_____

_____

_____

_____

_____

_____

_____

_____

_____

_____

_____

**Journal about whether you feel that you are a part of a really cool sister–hood type group.**
If you are not... would you want to be? And why?

_____

_____

_____

_____

_____

_____

_____

_____

_____

_____

_____

_____

_____

_____

_____

_____

_____

Even though sister-hood type friends have arguments, sometimes feelings get hurt or things go wrong, do you believe those group members basically trust, support and have respect for each other and for others?

_____

_____

_____

_____

_____

_____

_____

_____

_____

**Do you feel that you or someone you know are a part of a group that may not have that cool sister-hood feel?**

_____
_____
_____
_____
_____
_____
_____
_____
_____
_____
_____
_____
_____
_____
_____
_____
_____
_____
_____

Do you believe those group members basically trust, support and have respect for each other and for others?

_____
_____
_____
_____
_____
_____
_____
_____
_____
_____
_____
_____
_____

## Life Coaching

Open journal about whatever is in your heart today.
Remember to include the positive!

## Do you know of any girls that hurt others on purpose?
## Maybe some have even formed a clique?

It's been said that bullies & mean girls have been hurt and they use bullying to try to mask (cover up) the pain in their hearts. Some of their behaviors might include:

- Acting as though they are better than others • Gossiping or saying hurtful things about someone... maybe about their weight, or their clothing • Making snide comments • Insulting • Looking down upon others • Stealing friends • Excluding others • Stabbing others in the back • Spreading lies and rumors

Journal about any experiences you have had, or have witnessed that involved this type of behaviors.

_____
_____
_____
_____
_____
_____
_____
_____
_____
_____
_____
_____
_____
_____
_____
_____
_____
_____
_____
_____

Journal about how experiencing or witnessing the hurtful behaviors made you feel?

_____
_____
_____
_____
_____
_____
_____
_____
_____
_____
_____
_____
_____
_____
_____
_____
_____
_____
_____
_____
_____
_____
_____
_____
_____
_____
_____
_____
_____
_____
_____
_____

## Life Coaching

Open journal about whatever is in your heart today.
Remember to include the positive!

_____

_____

_____

_____

_____

_____

_____

_____

_____

_____

_____

_____

_____

_____

_____

_____

_____

_____

_____

_____

_____

_____

_____

_____

_____

_____

_____

_____

_____

_____

_____

_____

_____

_____

_____

Journal your feelings about whether you believe a 'mean' girl receives inner joy by making others feel unimportant and miserable. Why or why not?

_____

_____

_____

_____

_____

_____

_____

_____

_____

_____

_____

_____

_____

_____

_____

_____

_____

_____

_____

_____

_____

_____

_____

_____

_____

_____

_____

_____

_____

_____

_____

_____

## *Words Are Powerful*

What we say may affect the lives of others and unkind words may not only cause emotional pain, but as we see on the news, unkind words may also lead to death.

Kind words nurture and may even inspire change. We know the effects that kind and supportive words from coaches, grandparents, teachers, parents and others have on lives.

The use of negative words is like a maze and once we get drawn in it's hard to climb out, but we can break the negativity pattern by using kind and nurturing words which will generate a lasting word legacy that has the potential to carry on to the next generations.

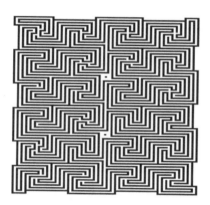

**Journal about whatever this brought to mind.**

_____

_____

_____

_____

_____

_____

## Life Coaching

"Where words leave off, music begins." — Heinrich Heine

Open journal about whatever is in your heart today.

Remember to include the positive!

_____

_____

_____

_____

_____

_____

_____

_____

_____

_____

_____

_____

_____

_____

_____

_____

_____

_____

_____

_____

_____

_____

_____

_____

_____

_____

_____

_____

_____

_____

# It's My Song

"Even in the mud and scum of things, something always, always sings."
— Ralph Waldo Emerson

The illustration on the next page represents three girls that you know. Pretend that you are a negative person and write some negative criticisms about them in the box below.

The second illustration represents you. Be very honest and in the box below, write negative self-talk things you have said to yourself.

---

Criticism of the girls:
_____
_____
_____

Criticism or negative self-talk of yourself:
_____
_____
_____

---

To illustrate the pain that negative self-talk does to others and to you.... when you finish writing, tear the illustration out of the journal and crumple it into the smallest ball that you can.

Once you have it as crumpled and as small as you can get it, you realize that your life has no place for such negative talk about others or about yourself and you are so sorry you said those things.

You want to take your words back.... so un-crumple and smooth out your picture. Get it as flat as possible to get rid of the words you wrote.

You now realize that tiny crumple lines remain... and that's what negative self-talk does... it leaves some degree of hurt and pain.

Blank

## Life Coaching

Open journal about whatever is in your heart today.
Remember to include the positive!

_____
_____
_____
_____
_____
_____
_____
_____
_____
_____
_____
_____
_____
_____
_____
_____
_____
_____
_____
_____
_____
_____
_____
_____
_____
_____
_____
_____
_____
_____
_____
_____
_____
_____

## Half Full or Half Empty? Optimistic or Pessimistic?
## Negative or Positive?

## Permeate Your Soul

Negativity not only eats at the essence of the negative person and her friends... it also eats into the heart of every group that negative people are associated with.

Who wants to be around a family, a classroom, a club, a team, a workplace, a church ... if they are saturated with negativity?

When non-smokers have spent a few minutes in a small space with people who smoke... the smoke permeates their hair and clothing and they can't get rid of the strong scent.

A similar thing happens when someone speaks negatively or gossips... or they read (or send) e-mails filled with gossip about others.... negativity permeates her heart.

Journal about what happens when positive-ness permeates your heart and you only speak words that are supportive and positive? ... you support others... you refuse to listen to negativity and gossip... you believe the best of others and you build others up?

_____
_____
_____
_____
_____
_____
_____
_____
_____
_____
_____
_____
_____
_____

## Life Coaching

Open journal about whatever is in your heart today.
Remember to include the positive!

Journal about what you feel are the differences between a sister-hood and a clique.

_____
_____
_____
_____
_____
_____
_____
_____
_____
_____
_____
_____
_____
_____
_____
_____
_____
_____
_____
_____
_____
_____
_____
_____
_____
_____

## Journal about why you think girls join cliques instead of joining a sister-hood.

## Life Coaching

Open journal about whatever is in your heart today.
Remember to include the positive!

## Your Response

In case you or someone you know becomes a target of a mean girl or clique, your best bet is to plan how you will respond to her efforts to make you upset.

Some suggestions might be very hard to pull off, but they include:
- don't let her know that your feelings are hurt
- don't run away crying
- act like you truly don't care (you do but don't let her see that)
- look bored say something like 'whatever'

Always tell a trusted adult if bullying puts you in physical danger; if it's affecting your grades or you don't want to go to school; if you feel sad or hopeless.

*Journal about what's in your heart.*

_____

_____

_____

_____

_____

_____

_____

_____

_____

_____

_____

_____

_____

_____

_____

_____

_____

_____

## Life Coaching

Open journal about whatever is in your heart today.
Remember to include the positive!

_____
_____
_____
_____
_____
_____
_____
_____
_____
_____
_____
_____
_____
_____
_____
_____
_____
_____
_____
_____
_____
_____
_____
_____
_____
_____
_____
_____
_____
_____
_____
_____
_____

## Drama Queen or Communication Reactions

When life doesn't go as planned, you actually get to choose how you respond to the problem. To get an outcome you want, you might use a tool of overreaction with tons of unnecessary drama queen reactions in order to get what you want, or to get someone to do something you want them to do.

On the other hand, to get an outcome you want, you might instead choose to react as a communication problem solver. Journal about ways that you think a communication problem solver might react to disappointments.

_____

_____

_____

_____

_____

_____

_____

_____

 If your mom said 'no' to something that was very important to you, journal your response about how would you choose to solve that problem with a:

Drama Queen Anger Reaction: Even though you may not be a drama queen problem solver….journal about what a drama-queen reaction might look like and sound like as you try to get your mom to do what you want.

_____

_____

_____

_____

_____

_____

_____

_____

Drama-Free, Communication Reaction: Even though you may not be a communication problem solver, journal about what your reaction might look like and sound like to get your mom to do what you want to do.

_____
_____
_____
_____
_____
_____
_____
_____
_____
_____

Journal about which type of problem solver do you believe earns respect from others?  And why?

_____
_____
_____
_____

Pick one time when you totally freaked out about something and journal about how you responded to the incidence.

_____
_____
_____
_____

Journal about how you could have reacted differently.

_____
_____
_____
_____

After you read the following questions... journal your thoughts. Think of someone you know that is a drama queen problem solver... have you ever noticed if she loses control only with certain people? Are there people in her life that she never has drama-queen reactions with? What might the differences in those people be? Maybe some expect the drama-queen reaction? Would some act as though they can't do anything about them? Do some expect you to respond as a communication problem solver? Would some never accept drama-queen reactions from you?

## *Building a Negative Free Community*

Now that you're starting to be aware of positive-ness, you may want to start creating a Negative Free Community…. in your self-talk, in your home, church, school, and other organizations.

A story in the Sept 2007 Positive Thinking: Attitude is Everything Magazine tells how a little green rubber band helped to change a woman's life. Susan was not aware of how deep her self-negativity was until her physical trainer told her that she noticed that she was very down on herself.

The trainer had Susan wear a green rubber band on her wrist… to snap each time she put herself down, which helped Susan to realize just how many times she put herself down. She realized that she needed to make a conscious effort to be kind & forgiving to herself. The rubber band helped her gain a whole new outlook.

You are invited to wear not only one rubber band on your wrist for two weeks… but wear two different colored rubber bands to help break negative habits.

The first band is to snap your wrist when you have negative thoughts and self-talk about yourself… or you put yourself down in any way. Snap your wrist rather hard and then replace the negative thought with a positive one. Example… "I'm so dumb…". SNAP WRIST. Then replace the negative with a positive… "I'm creative… "

The other band is to snap your wrist when you think negative thoughts or when you are complaining about someone else. Snap your wrist and replace your negative thoughts about the person with positive thoughts.

Once you start recognizing just how often you have negative thoughts or criticize yourself and others… then you can start to change those habits. The rubber band exercise is a good one to share with other people in your family, school, church or organizations, and together you can work to create a Negative Free Community.

**Journal about any additional actions you might take to make your self-talk and your environment more positive.**

## Life Coaching

"Music in the soul can be heard by the universe." — Lao Tzu
Open journal about whatever is in your heart today.
Remember to include the positive!

## Inspiration

*"Kindness in words creates confidence. Kindness in thinking creates profoundness. Kindness in giving creates love."* — Lao Tzu

Think about that someone who had encouraged and inspired you. It could be a parent, a relative, a teacher, a coach or a friend. That person may have inspired you by making you feel important. That person may have spoken positive words, or it could have been their actions that encouraged you and you know you will carry the memories with you for all of your life.

**Journal about your experiences and the effect it had on your life.**

_____
_____
_____
_____
_____
_____
_____
_____
_____
_____
_____
_____
_____
_____
_____
_____
_____
_____
_____
_____
_____
_____
_____
_____

Journal your inspirational person a thank you …. thanking him or her for what they did for you and what effect they had on your life. You might want to transfer your note to a card and send it to the person. Write the note even if the person has passed away. It doesn't have to be long or complicated. But it can be.

## Life Coaching

"Music is the language of the spirit.
It opens the secret of life bringing peace, abolishing strife."
— Kahlil Gibran
Open journal about whatever is in your heart today.
Remember to include the positive!

_____
_____
_____
_____
_____
_____
_____
_____
_____
_____
_____
_____
_____
_____
_____
_____
_____
_____
_____
_____
_____
_____
_____
_____
_____
_____
_____
_____
_____
_____

## Protection From Cyberspace Bullies

**You may have heard this a hundred times, but to keep safe:**

Never give out personal details such as your name, address, school, phone number, your age, gender or location.

Don't accept any offers of money or presents, even free offers.

Unless you have your parent's permission and they accompany you, do not meet with anyone you have met on the Internet.

Don't share passwords, even with your best friends.

Don't reply to anything that is abusive or obscene. You or your parents can contact your server to report it.

When bullied, save & print out everything (but don't keep reading it) that's being said about you in case it is ever needed.

**Journal about additional ways to protect yourself.**

_____
_____
_____
_____
_____
_____
_____
_____
_____
_____
_____
_____
_____
_____
_____

## What Matters?

*What lies behind us and what lies ahead of us are tiny matters compared to what lives within us.* --Henry David Thoreau

Journal about what things in your life matter most right now?

_____
_____
_____
_____
_____
_____
_____
_____
_____
_____

What age have you found to be your best age... so far... and why?

_____
_____
_____
_____
_____
_____

What are some of the funniest things that have happened to you?

_____
_____
_____
_____
_____
_____
_____
_____

## *Singing Solo - Life-Roles*

We all have life-roles in many areas of our lives, such as in our family, at school, in our groups, in our friendships, at church, at play, in our community or in our social lives. In some of our areas, we may have several roles such as in a family—you may be a daughter, sister, cousin and so on.

List as many life-roles as you can think of in your life.

1. _____     2. _____
3. _____     4. _____
5. _____     6. _____
7. _____     8. _____
9. _____     10. _____
11. _____     12. _____

_____
_____
_____

Journal about your feelings about two of your roles that you absolutely love.

_____
_____
_____
_____
_____
_____
_____
_____
_____
_____
_____
_____
_____
_____
_____

# Life Coaching

Open journal about whatever is in your heart today.
Remember to include the positive!

---
---
---
---
---
---
---
---
---
---
---
---
---
---
---
---
---
---
---
---
---
---
---
---
---
---
---
---
---
---
---
---
---
---
---
---
---
---

## *Life-Role Leadership*

*"If your actions inspire others to dream more, learn more, do more and become more, you are a leader."* -John Quincy Adams

In your life-roles that you previously identified, go back and place a (√) check by each role that you can identify that requires leadership responsibilities.

Select three of those roles and journal positive ways that you can communicate to others, so that their self-worth is enhanced. (An example might be: as a sister or as a babysitter I can _____).

_____
_____
_____
_____
_____
_____
_____
_____
_____
_____
_____
_____
_____
_____

Describe at least three benefits that you personally receive by communicating in a positive way.

_____
_____
_____
_____
_____
_____

## *Leadership*

Some think that leadership is reserved solely for those in management positions; however, we are all leaders in some of our life roles. You may very well provide leadership in some of your other roles that you did not place a checkmark on. For example... in your group you may have someone that the group sees as the leader and you may feel that you do not have any leadership duties. You may not be the appointed leader, however... you do have co-group members and you may provide leadership roles for them at times.

If you think about it... you probably provide some type of leadership at times in each of your personal roles. Take a moment to review your roles and add checkmarks if you now feel you do provide leadership in other roles.

Journal about those additional leadership roles:

_____
_____
_____
_____
_____
_____
_____
_____
_____
_____
_____
_____
_____
_____
_____
_____
_____
_____
_____

## *Leadership Style*

*"Leaders instill in their people a hope for success and a belief in themselves. Positive leaders empower people to accomplish their goals."*
*–Unknown*

Many books and DVDs are devoted to the topic of leadership and most describe leadership styles that range from dominating to empowering. How do you see yourself as a leader?

_____
_____
_____
_____
_____
_____

What are your personality characteristics that you bring to your role as leader and how do they help you to be an effective leader?

_____
_____
_____
_____
_____
_____

Describe your leadership style's strengths and weaknesses and journal about any steps you may take to become a more effective leader.

_____
_____
_____
_____
_____
_____
_____
_____

## Life Coaching

"Life is like music; it must be composed by ear, feeling, and instinct, not by rule." – Samuel Butler

Open journal about whatever is in your heart today.

Remember to include the positive!

## Purpose?

"It is this mission of the dancer to contribute to the betterment of all mankind." - Ruth St. Denis

Write whatever comes to mind to the questions:

What is my dream for the world?

_____
_____
_____
_____
_____
_____
_____
_____
_____

What is the most awesome thing I could do for the world?

_____
_____
_____
_____
_____
_____
_____

At this moment in my life, I believe my purpose is (1)

_____
_____
_____

What is my purpose? (2)        (It can be the same or different).

_____
_____
_____

What is my purpose? (3)          (It can be the same or different).

_____
_____
_____


What is my purpose? (4)          (It can be the same or different).

_____
_____
_____
_____


Seriously.... from all of my responses ....my purpose is...

_____
_____
_____
_____
_____
_____
_____
_____
_____
_____
_____
_____
_____
_____
_____
_____
_____
_____
_____
_____
_____
_____
_____

# Life Coaching

Open journal about whatever is in your heart today.
Remember to include the positive!

## Media and Body Image

Peer pressure and media pressure play a big role in influencing teens about body image. You are surrounded by media images of super-slim teen celebrities, fashion models, beauty and diet commercials and they all work together to convince you to not only buy products but also to see them as the norm.

Journal about ways you can combat the advertising tactics that media use to manipulate you into believing that your looks, body shape and size determine success and happiness.

## Distorted View?

Do you think that maybe the media affects the way you see yourself?
Journal about the possibility that those images help to give you a
distorted view of yourself when you look in your mirror.

_____
_____
_____
_____
_____
_____
_____
_____
_____
_____
_____
_____
_____
_____
_____
_____
_____
_____
_____
_____
_____
_____
_____
_____
_____
_____
_____
_____
_____

## Life Coaching

Open journal about whatever is in your heart today.
Remember to include the positive!

_____
_____
_____
_____
_____
_____
_____
_____
_____
_____
_____
_____
_____
_____
_____
_____
_____
_____
_____
_____
_____
_____
_____
_____
_____
_____
_____
_____
_____
_____
_____
_____
_____

## Body Image and Real Women and Real Teen Celebrities.

Media manipulates by using advertisements that set impossible standards but there are many celebrities who are not super-slim and they represent real women and teens. Some of them include:  Adele, Beyonce, Christina Aguilera, Christina Hendricks, Drew Barrymore, Jennifer Hudson, Jennifer Lopez, Jennifer Love Hewitt, Jessica Alba, Jessica Biel, Jessica Simpson, Kelly Clarkson, Kim Kardashian, Mariah Carey, Renee Sellweger, Rihanna, Scarlett Johansson, Tyra Banks.

Journal about what this brings to mind.

_____

_____

_____

_____

_____

_____

_____

_____

_____

_____

_____

_____

_____

_____

_____

_____

_____

_____

_____

_____

_____

_____

_____

_____

_____

_____

_____

**Below, write the names of four women or teens that you know and admire that are of average size or larger.**

List characteristics (besides beauty) that make them attractive.

Journal about the inner personal qualities that make for true success... instead of physical looks.

# Life Coaching

"If I were not a physicist, I would probably be a musician. I often think in music. I live my daydreams in music. I see my life in terms of music." — Albert Einstein

Open journal about whatever is in your heart today.

Remember to include the positive!

_____
_____
_____
_____
_____
_____
_____
_____
_____
_____
_____
_____
_____
_____
_____
_____
_____
_____
_____
_____
_____
_____
_____
_____
_____
_____
_____
_____
_____
_____

**Teen body image is also influenced by peers.**

In an effort to fit in, teens may feel pressured by peers to look a certain way. If her peers won't allow her to fit in their crowd because of her body size, she may become a victim of bullying and teasing.

**Journal about whatever is in your heart.**

**Singing in the Rain**

**Adapted from Mayo Clinic**
Healthy body image: Tips for guiding girls

**Help establish healthy eating habits.** Exercise and eat a healthy
diet for your health, not just to look a certain way.
**Counter negative media messages.** Think about what you
read and watch as well as the products you buy.
**Value what you do**, rather than what you look like.
Praise your efforts, skills and achievements.
**Physical activity.** Participating in physical activities — particularly
those that don't emphasize a particular weight or body shape —
can help promote good self-esteem and a positive body image.

http://www.mayoclinic.com/health/healthy-body-image/MY01225

**Journal about what's in your heart.**

_____

_____

_____

_____

_____

_____

_____

_____

_____

_____

_____

_____

_____

_____

_____

_____

_____

## Life Coaching

Open journal about whatever is in your heart today.
Remember to include the positive!

_____
_____
_____
_____
_____
_____
_____
_____
_____
_____
_____
_____
_____
_____
_____
_____
_____
_____
_____
_____
_____
_____
_____
_____
_____
_____
_____
_____
_____
_____
_____
_____
_____

## Loneliness

Loneliness isn't about being alone.... It's about feeling alone. Sometimes it's feeling lonely even when you're with people, especially when you're with someone that you don't really want to be with. Some steps to combat loneliness & shyness might feel like risks but they're worth trying regardless of how hard they are:

- Make sure to always lead with a smile to show that you are a positive, warm and confident person.
- Recognize loneliness as the temporary feeling it is and use your support system to work through it. Try to start each day saying 'hi' to at least one person that you might not normally say 'hi' to.
- Make yourself do something social that you normally wouldn't do... possibly an after-school activity; join a club or church youth group; attend a meeting.
- Build your positive self-esteem further by using tools such as this journal that will help you to be more self-confident.
- Most of all.... respect yourself even when you're feeling lonely or shy.
- Always seek help whenever any feelings become depression.

**Journal about other possibilities that may help when dealing with loneliness.**

_____
_____
_____
_____
_____
_____
_____
_____
_____
_____
_____
_____
_____
_____
_____
_____

# Life Coaching

Open journal about whatever is in your heart today.
Remember to include the positive!

_____

_____

_____

_____

_____

_____

_____

_____

_____

_____

_____

_____

_____

_____

_____

_____

_____

_____

_____

_____

_____

_____

_____

_____

_____

_____

_____

_____

_____

_____

_____

_____

## May I Have This Risk?

The *Teens Today* 2004 research identified three broad categories of positive risk-taking. http://www.sadd.org/teenstoday/survey04.htm

**Life Risks**
Social – e.g. joining a club or group
Emotional – e.g. asking someone on a date or sharing feelings with friends
Physical – e.g. rock climbing

**School Risks**
Academic – e.g. taking an advanced placement course
Athletic – e.g. trying out for a sports team
Extracurricular – e.g. running for student council

**Community Risks**
Volunteering – e.g. helping the elderly or homeless
Mentoring – e.g. working with younger children
Leading – e.g. starting a business or charity

The biggest positive risk I ever took was...

_____
_____
_____
_____

The positive risk I most regret not taking is...

_____
_____
_____
_____
_____

*Twenty years from now you will be more disappointed by the things you didn't do than by the ones you did. So throw off the bowlines, sail away from the safe harbor, catch the trade winds in your sails. Explore. Dream. Discover.*
*– Mark Twain*

# Life Coaching

Open journal about whatever is in your heart today.
Remember to include the positive!

_____
_____
_____
_____
_____
_____
_____
_____
_____
_____
_____
_____
_____
_____
_____
_____
_____
_____
_____
_____
_____
_____
_____
_____
_____
_____
_____
_____
_____
_____
_____
_____
_____

## *Fear*

*"We have to start teaching ourselves not to be afraid."*
*-William Faulkner*

Fear often plays a role in the various areas of our lives: school, future plans, dating, relationships, and emotional areas. We may fear failure, success, emotional or physical pain, the unknown, our lack of capabilities…. and the list goes on.

We often feel fear when we start to step up to meet challenges or when we start to make changes in our lives. As we start to move out of our comfort zone, we may start to fear what 'might' happen and then our fear may limit our decisions or our plans.

At this point, give your greatest fears names. Start with your greatest fear and list all that you can think of.
(Rejection-Success-Being Wrong-Failure-Confrontation… whatever).

_____

_____

_____

_____

_____

_____

_____

_____

_____

_____

_____

_____

_____

_____

_____

_____

_____

_____

## Life Coaching

Open journal about whatever is in your heart today.
Remember to include the positive!

## Sailing Ships

*"I am not afraid of storms, for I am learning how to sail my ship."* -Louisa May Alcott

If you experience fear as you step up to meet a challenge, you might acknowledge the fear; allow yourself to briefly feel the fear and then remind yourself that it's really ok. You may discover that it may even be 'normal' to feel fear when you begin to make changes in your life.

Journal about a fear that you might face as you step up to make a change in your life. What are the worst possible things that could happen if you step up? What steps come to mind that might help you to come to terms with that fear?

_____

_____

_____

_____

_____

_____

_____

_____

_____

_____

_____

_____

_____

_____

_____

_____

_____

_____

_____

_____

_____

## Life Coaching

Open journal about whatever is in your heart today.
Remember to include the positive!

## *Self- Harming Masks*

Self-harming behaviors are used to numb, but the behaviors are also masks to hide behind. Almost any behavior can be used as a mask and some examples include: bitterness, being critical, eating disorders, gambling, gossiping, lying, self-mutilation, sex addictions, spending problems, stealing, body image problems, control issues, fear, guilt, shame, impatience, people pleasing, perfectionism, procrastination, smoking, alcohol, drug abuse, anger, and the list goes on.

There are times that our experiences of some type of trauma led to self-harming activities and you may want to read the following that is written in the first person as it applies to you and/or you may share it with someone you know who has experienced trauma.

"I know that I have spent years stuck in my rut of self-harming behaviors and I do not want to continue in this dead end direction.

I am learning that many girls share a common history of some type of trauma and pain that leaves a hole in our heart and I am one of them. The trauma left me feeling that I am somehow broken and that I am different than other teens. I had no choice but to be strong... and I tried to fill the hole in my heart by myself by playing sports, video games and by constantly reading ... but in the end... the hole remained.

After discovering my self-harming mask.... I used it as a way to lessen my pain. My self-harming activities created what I believed to be an inner place of safety... but I was wrong... it became my maze and I couldn't find my way out.

My self-harming behavior...was supposed to help me feel loved. But it never did... and I developed an even greater need for a constant supply of my activity... until it became the most important thing in my life.

In this process of self-harming activity, over time...my TRUE SELF... the 'me in me' eroded into a FALSE SELF that is no longer 'me'.

Now that I am coming to understand the truth about the relationship of trauma and pain to my self-harming behavior, I am ready to face the hole in my heart squarely.

With this journal, I am taking my heart out of my closet and I will dance with it. In order to truly live life, I will create new steps and a new song that will lead to healing.

I will continue on a path of journaling and I will search for other opportunities to guide me in the process of replacing my FALSE SELF with my very real AUTHENTIC SELF. I will not be afraid to ask adults I trust or counselors for help".

Journal whatever this has brought to your mind.

_____
_____
_____
_____
_____
_____
_____
_____
_____
_____
_____
_____
_____
_____
_____
_____
_____
_____
_____
_____
_____
_____
_____
_____

# Life Coaching

Open journal about whatever is in your heart today.
Remember to include the positive!

_____

_____

_____

_____

_____

_____

_____

_____

_____

_____

_____

_____

_____

_____

_____

_____

_____

_____

_____

_____

_____

_____

_____

_____

_____

_____

_____

_____

_____

_____

## *Self-Soothing*

When we are in emotional distress and we want to feel better, healthy self-soothing brings comfort in a positive way because self-soothing is about comfort instead of numbing.

Some examples of self-soothing include:
• Listening to music • Singing • Wrapping yourself in a warm blanket • Hugging a pet • Rocking in a rocking chair or swing • Walking • Making your bath cozy • Taking a SPA bath with nice soaps and body washes

You may recall your efforts as a younger child to sooth yourself. Some have blankets and some suck their thumb. Since self-soothing is unique to each person, journal about ways you self-soothed yourself in the past; what you do now; and maybe identify some new techniques you may use in the future.

_____
_____
_____
_____
_____
_____
_____
_____
_____
_____
_____
_____
_____
_____
_____
_____
_____
_____
_____
_____
_____

## Life Coaching

Open journal about whatever is in your heart today.
Remember to include the positive!

_____
_____
_____
_____
_____
_____
_____
_____
_____
_____
_____
_____
_____
_____
_____
_____
_____
_____
_____
_____
_____
_____
_____
_____
_____
_____
_____
_____
_____
_____
_____
_____
_____
_____

## *Injustices And Grudges*

Have you ever thought that you might like to have a better sense of your self-worth or self-esteem? Sometimes low self-worth is caused, at least in-part, because you were hurt or treated unfairly by someone in your family... or at school... in your church... in a social organization... or in other relationships. Maybe you have been hurt by several people. Maybe you have hurt yourself.

Perhaps there were injustices you witnessed or experienced... maybe earlier in childhood... maybe last year... or yesterday. Maybe you internalized the pain and kept your hurt private and close to your heart.

There may be grudges that you are not ready to let go but if there are any... then journal from the heart about any injustices or conflicts that you experienced that you are now ready to put into words.

_____

_____

_____

_____

_____

_____

_____

_____

_____

_____

_____

_____

_____

_____

_____

_____

_____

_____

_____

_____

## Life Coaching

Open journal about whatever is in your heart today.
Remember to include the positive!

## *Unresolved Grudges*

If you have pain from an injustice that has never had a resolution... it remains an open wound that can never heal.... and your heart remains stuck. You might leave and find another school or church... maybe even join a different club or organization... you might not speak to the person again... but since you have not resolved the issue... you remain emotionally stuck.

Journal about what's in your heart.

_____

_____

_____

_____

_____

_____

_____

_____

_____

_____

_____

_____

_____

_____

_____

_____

_____

_____

_____

_____

_____

_____

_____

_____

_____

_____

_____

_____

# Life Coaching

Open journal about whatever is in your heart today.
Remember to include the positive!

_____
_____
_____
_____
_____
_____
_____
_____
_____
_____
_____
_____
_____
_____
_____
_____
_____
_____
_____
_____
_____
_____
_____
_____
_____
_____
_____
_____
_____
_____
_____

## 'Letting It Go' Activity

This activity is not intended for those with severe trauma or circumstances that require professional counseling.

If you have an injustice that is unresolved and you are ready to let it go and release the hold it has on your heart... this forgiveness activity can guide you to let it go.

Read the entire exercise and then gather several stones or other small items and place them on a table in front of you and then sit down and relax.

READ as if your Life Coach is reading to you:
"I forgive" are only words and true inner peace cannot come if you only say the words but do not truly let it go in your heart. You can forgive... without condoning the person's behavior. Sometimes we think we forgive someone... then we take it back and it starts all over again.

You may be hardest on yourself for the pain you inflicted on yourself or on others. Perhaps you caused pain as a child or now in your adolescence. You might have guilt and shame about your actions ... and maybe it's your time to forgive yourself... to let it go once and for all.

If you are ready to forgive yourself ... then ....select a small stone or a similar object and hold it in your fingers as you sit quietly and then slowly read the following in the first person.

A grudge is a heavy burden that has created a small hole in my heart. Forgiving... or letting it go... will help me to fill that hole. I am not condoning my behaviors, but I have decided to forgive myself for my behaviors and to let them go.

(Visualize your face on your stone.) So many times I forgive.... and then I forget and bring back the old negative feelings. This time I am truly ready to move on.... and to let it go completely... once and for all.

This is a new moment... I am free to let go. I am releasing all the hurtful injustices I committed; my regrets; my 'what ifs'. I forgive me whether I feel that I deserve it or not. It's time. I release myself from prison.... I am safe.... I am free...

*Take several slow deep breaths and blow out.... releasing the pain from the injustices... releasing the poison ... releasing the anger... the negativity... the guilt... the shame.*

*Breathe in the positive with "I deserve love.... joy..... courage.... peace..... serenity."*
*Breathe in and fill the hole in your heart with "I accept love.... joy.... courage.... peace..... serenity.... and I accept them now."*

*Take a few moments to close your eyes and visualize yourself after releasing yourself from prison. Visualize yourself through a picture window. Watch yourself as you now move and act with complete inner confidence and freedom. Visualize your face that now exudes joy, peace and serenity. Visualize your heart as whole.*

**Journal about whatever is in your heart.**

_____
_____
_____
_____
_____
_____
_____
_____
_____
_____
_____
_____
_____
_____
_____
_____
_____
_____
_____
_____
_____
_____

## Life Coaching

Open journal about whatever is in your heart today.
Remember to include the positive!

_____

_____

_____

_____

_____

_____

_____

_____

_____

_____

_____

_____

_____

_____

_____

_____

_____

_____

_____

_____

_____

_____

_____

_____

_____

_____

_____

_____

_____

## *And Now the Others*

"The best thing to give to your enemy is forgiveness....."
— Benjamin Franklin

If you have experienced injustices committed by others and they remain unresolved and you are ready to release the hold they have on your heart... this same forgiveness activity can guide you to let them go.

"I forgive" are only words and true inner peace cannot come if you only say the words but do not truly let it go in your heart. You can forgive... without condoning the person's behavior. Sometimes we think we forgive someone... then we take it back and it starts all over again.

If there are others who inflicted pain on you... perhaps when you were a child or now as an adolescent, and you are now ready to let them go. Maybe it's your time to let them truly go once and for all.

If you are ready to forgive ... then ....select a small stone one by one for each person that you are ready to forgive. Hold them in your fingers as you sit quietly and then slowly read the following.

A grudge is a heavy burden to bear. It has created a small hole in your heart and forgiving... or letting it go... will help to fill that hole. You are not condoning their behaviors, but you have decided to forgive them for their behaviors and to let them go.

Visualize each face on your separate stones one by one. So many times you forgive.... and then forget and bring back the old negative feelings. This time you are truly ready to move on.... and to let them go completely... once and for all.  Read the following in the first person.

This is a new moment... I am free to let go. I am releasing all of the hurtful injustices each has committed. I forgive each of them whether I feel that they deserve it or not. It's time. I release myself from prison.... I am safe.... I am free...

*Take a deep breath and blow out…. releasing the pain from the injustices… releasing the poison … releasing the anger… the negativity…*

*Breathe in the positive with "I deserve love…. joy….. courage…. peace….. serenity."*

*Breathe in and fill the hole in your heart with "I accept love…. joy…. courage…. peace….. serenity…. and I accept them now."*

*Take a few moments to close your eyes and visualize your relaxed face after releasing yourself from prison. Visualize yourself as free… and your face now exudes joy, courage, peace and serenity. Visualize your heart as whole.*

_____

_____

_____

_____

_____

_____

_____

_____

_____

_____

_____

_____

_____

Journal about whatever is in your heart.

_____

_____

_____

_____

_____

_____

_____

_____

_____

_____

_____

_____

_____

## Life Coaching

Open journal about whatever is in your heart today.
Remember to include the positive!

## Your Vision Statement

Go confidently in the direction of your dreams. Live the life you have imagined.
--Henry David Thoreau

Most experts say that to make a personal vision statement, it's important to look down our life-road and envision what we want our future to look like....what kind of life we want to have.

Of course our minds cannot actually tell us what our future will be... but we can use our imagination to visualize who we want to be and what we want our futures to look like.

As your Life Coach, you are going to do a visualization exercise... to imagine your future.

**Read the following and then close your eyes lead yourself through the exercise.**
Take a moment to focus. Take slow deep breaths and relax.
With your eyes closed... Imagine that you are looking out of a picture window....
Imagine a time in your future...50, 60, 70 years from now.
Imagine that you are no longer on earth and your friends and family have gathered to honor your life.

As you look out that window.... Visualize yourself in that room with your family and friends.
As they each stand and speak about you....what would you like them to be able to say about your life?

Visualize with vivid details your answer to the following questions.
What are you known for?
What types of things did you do?
What kind of family person did you become?
What types of things have become important to you?
How did you treat others?
What have you accomplished?
What new skill have you learned?
How does it feel to be an authentic person?

Open your eyes and relax.

## Life Coaching

Open journal about whatever is in your heart today.
Remember to include the positive!

_____
_____
_____
_____
_____
_____
_____
_____
_____
_____
_____
_____
_____
_____
_____
_____
_____
_____
_____
_____
_____
_____
_____
_____
_____
_____
_____
_____
_____
_____
_____
_____
_____

## My Vision Statement

A vision statement is typically about a paragraph long and it is a statement of who you want to become. This is your statement and there is no right or wrong. Use the vision you imagined to write your vision statement.

_____

_____

_____

_____

_____

_____

_____

_____

_____

_____


Now, as you start to compare your current life with your vision for your future life, you may notice that you need to make some adjustments in order to finish your life-song on your terms. Journal about any changes or adjustments that you feel you may have to start making and share your thoughts about where your vision statement will lead you in your future.

_____

_____

_____

_____

_____

_____

_____

_____

_____

_____

_____

_____

_____

# Life Coaching

Open journal about whatever is in your heart today.
Remember to include the positive!

_____
_____
_____
_____
_____
_____
_____
_____
_____
_____
_____
_____
_____
_____
_____
_____
_____
_____
_____
_____
_____
_____
_____
_____
_____
_____
_____
_____
_____
_____
_____

*"The only person you are destined to become is the person you decide to be."* — Ralph Waldo Emerson

There are many books and articles telling us that it's not only companies that have brands, but that we each have a personal brand. Our brand is what comes to mind to others when they hear our name. It's our reputation.

Personal branding is the process of discovering what is true and unique about ourselves that helps us to stand out in a crowd.

Branding is not about changing who you are, but it is about becoming more of who you are by discovering... or re-discovering your true authentic self.

How do you describe each person's reputation when you hear the name Justin Bieber? President Obama? Miley Cyrus? Jamie Foxx? Betty White? Michelle Obama? Oprah?   Beyonce?   Your Mother?

Like them or not... we do have an opinion because their brands show in nearly everything they say and do.

It's important that we build our own brand before someone else does. Think about how often kids get teased by name-calling and then those words become the kid's brand. Words like loser and fat, do not reflect anyone's true inner self.  Has anyone ever branded you with qualities that did not reflect your true self?

_____
_____
_____
_____
_____
_____
_____

# Life Coaching

Open journal about whatever is in your heart today.
Remember to include the positive!

_____
_____
_____
_____
_____
_____
_____
_____
_____
_____
_____
_____
_____
_____
_____
_____
_____
_____
_____
_____
_____
_____
_____
_____
_____
_____
_____
_____
_____
_____
_____
_____

**The next few journaling pages will help you to start to define or to re-define your brand.**

Describe yourself (your reputation...your brand) the way you see yourself.

_____
_____
_____
_____
_____
_____
_____

Describe yourself (your reputation...your brand) the way you believe your friends and family would.

_____
_____
_____
_____
_____
_____

Our personal brands reflect our true character, and they are built on our core values, strengths and our personal distinctiveness.

### *Core Values*

Your values are the essence of what you believe in and what motivates you to act. They reflect who you are at this point in your life and they serve as an inner compass that guides your life and your experiences. Your values represent what is unique about you and they are reflected ... in everything you think.... say.... and ... do.

A good start to create or redefine your brand is to identify the core values that help you live your life and are important to your personal brand.

## VALUES THAT HELP US LIVE OUR LIVES

___ APPRECIATION     ___ FAMILY     ___ FRIENDSHIP

___ HEALTH     ___ INTEGRITY     ___ LOVE

___ POLITE     ___ RESPONSIBLE     ___ TOLERANCE

___ UNITY     ___ COMPASSION     ___ FAIRNESS

___ FORGIVENESS     ___ GENEROSITY     ___ HONESTY

___ KINDNESS     ___ LOYALTY     ___ RELIABLE

___ SELF-DISCIPLINE     ___ TRUSTWORTHY     ___ WISDOM

___ COOPERATION     ___ FAITH     ___ FREEDOM

___ HARMONY     ___ HUMOR     ___ HELPING OTHERS

___ RESPECT     ___ SHARING     ___ TRUTH

___ FAITHFULNESS     ___FORWARD LOOKING     ___ COMMUNITY

___ CARING     ___ CALM     ___ DETERMINED

___ DECENT     ___ EMPOWERED     ___ PEACEFUL

___ PATIENT     ___ PERSISTENT     ___ POSITIVE

___SINCERITY     ___POWERFUL     ___RISK TAKING

___RESPECT     ___RESOURCEFUL     ___ SELF-ESTEEM

___SELF-EXPRESSION     ___SENSITIVITY     ___SERVICE

Don't be limited by the list, add other values that feel right for you.

_____

_____

Circle 15 that apply to you at this time in your life and then spend time tonight just thinking about and reviewing this list.

## CORE VALUES

| | | |
|---|---|---|
| ___ APPRECIATION | ___ FAMILY | ___ FRIENDSHIP |
| ___ HEALTH | ___ INTEGRITY | ___ LOVE |
| ___ POLITE | ___ RESPONSIBLE | ___ TOLERANCE |
| ___ UNITY | ___ COMPASSION | ___ FAIRNESS |
| ___ FORGIVENESS | ___ GENEROSITY | ___ HONESTY |
| ___ KINDNESS | ___ LOYALTY | ___ RELIABLE |
| ___ SELF-DISCIPLINE | ___ TRUSTWORTHY | ___ WISDOM |
| ___ COOPERATION | ___ FAITH | ___ FREEDOM |
| ___ HARMONY | ___ HUMOR | ___ HELPING OTHERS |
| ___ RESPECT | ___ SHARING | ___ TRUTH |
| ___ FAITHFULNESS | ___ FORWARD LOOKING | ___ COMMUNITY |
| ___ CARING | ___ CALM | ___ DETERMINED |
| ___ DECENT | ___ EMPOWERED | ___ PEACEFUL |
| ___ PATIENT | ___ PERSISTENT | ___ POSITIVE |
| ___ SINCERITY | ___ POWERFUL | ___ RISK TAKING |
| ___ RESPECT | ___ RESOURCEFUL | ___ SELF-ESTEEM |
| ___ SELF-EXPRESSION | ___ SENSITIVITY | ___ SERVICE |

After thinking about the values you circled previously, review them again here and circle 15 that apply to you at this time in your life. They may or may not be the same.

Add the other values that you added previously or add new ones that now feel right for you.

_____

_____

# Life Coaching

Open journal about whatever is in your heart today.
Remember to include the positive!

_____

_____

_____

_____

_____

_____

_____

_____

_____

_____

_____

_____

_____

_____

_____

_____

_____

_____

_____

_____

_____

_____

_____

_____

_____

_____

_____

_____

## *Clarifying Your Core Values*

"Make the most of yourself....for that is all there is of you."
— Ralph Waldo Emerson

Of the values listed, did you find some that instantly jolted you and you immediately circled them?

_____
_____
_____
_____
_____
_____

Did you find other values that you just had to circle?

_____
_____
_____
_____
_____
_____

Did you find some that are a priority, yet sometimes you neglect them?

_____
_____
_____
_____
_____
_____
_____

## Life Coaching

Open journal about whatever is in your heart today.
Remember to include the positive!

_____
_____
_____
_____
_____
_____
_____
_____
_____
_____
_____
_____
_____
_____
_____
_____
_____
_____
_____
_____
_____
_____
_____
_____
_____
_____
_____
_____
_____
_____
_____
_____
_____

## *Prioritizing Your Core Values*

From your list, decide which 10 values are uniquely the most important to you. List those values with your least important value at the bottom and end with your most important value at the top. Add notes to your selections in order to remind yourself of your thinking process in the future when you return to read your journal.

You may combine two or three values with slashes on the same line as long as they fit together such as (honesty/Integrity/truthfulness).

| Priority | Core Values | Thoughts-Reflections |
|---|---|---|
| 1 | | |
| 2 | | |
| 3 | | |
| 4 | | |
| 5 | | |
| 6 | | |
| 7 | | |
| 8 | | |
| 9 | | |
| 10 | | |
| | | |

# Life Coaching

Open journal about whatever is in your heart today.
Remember to include the positive!

**Strengths and Weaknesses** are internal and along with your core values, they help to identify your brand.

Describe your strengths:

_____
_____
_____
_____
_____
_____

Describe your weaknesses:

_____
_____
_____
_____
_____
_____

Journal about how your strengths have impacted your life

_____
_____
_____
_____
_____
_____
_____
_____
_____
_____
_____
_____

# Life Coaching

Open journal about whatever is in your heart today.
Remember to include the positive!

_____

_____

_____

_____

_____

_____

_____

_____

_____

_____

_____

_____

_____

_____

_____

_____

_____

_____

_____

_____

_____

_____

_____

_____

_____

_____

_____

_____

_____

_____

_____

## Life Passions

*Curtain! Fast music! Light! Ready for the last finale! Great! The show looks good, the show looks good!* Florenz Ziegfeld

Now, let's move to your life passions that are more of an outer symbol that makes it easier for others to see who you are because your passions show your personality. Passions are your interests and the things you love to do.

Journal about your passions that you love and help to make you…. you.

_____
_____
_____
_____
_____
_____
_____
_____
_____
_____
_____
_____
_____
_____
_____
_____
_____
_____
_____
_____
_____
_____
_____
_____
_____

## Life Coaching

Open journal about whatever is in your heart today.
Remember to include the positive!

_____

_____

_____

_____

_____

_____

_____

_____

_____

_____

_____

_____

_____

_____

_____

_____

_____

_____

_____

_____

_____

_____

_____

_____

_____

_____

_____

_____

_____

_____

_____

_____

_____

_____

## Talents and Skills.

*"The greatest thing a man can do in this world is to make the most possible out of the stuff that has been given him. This is success, and there is no other."* — Orison Swett Marden Learn to Expect a Great Deal of Life

Another important part of your brand that helps set you apart includes your talents and your skills. What are you really good at? What skills make you special or unique? Don't forget to include skills and talents you use in school or in your other life roles.

You might want to ask family and friends what talents or skills that they see in you now or in your past. Journal about your talents and skills.

_____

_____

_____

_____

_____

_____

_____

_____

_____

_____

_____

_____

_____

_____

_____

_____

_____

_____

_____

_____

_____

_____

## Write Your Brand Description

Review your journal worksheets and use your strongest characteristics, values, passions and talents to describe the image of the brand of 'you' that you want to project to others. (Think about Nike as an example. What image do they project to the public in everything they say and do?)_____

_____
_____
_____
_____
_____
_____

Now, from your brand description-- reduce it to a tagline of few words that provides the punch to your brand. (For Nike it is: Just do it)

_____
_____
_____

Brand Projection --With your personality, attitudes, body language and style, how will you project your brand through your thoughts, your words, your behaviors and your actions to others?

_____
_____
_____
_____
_____
_____
_____

How does having an authentic defined brand make you feel?

_____
_____
_____
_____

## Life Coaching

Open journal about whatever is in your heart today.
Remember to include the positive!

_____
_____
_____
_____
_____
_____
_____
_____
_____
_____
_____
_____
_____
_____
_____
_____
_____
_____
_____
_____
_____
_____
_____
_____
_____
_____
_____
_____
_____
_____
_____
_____
_____

## Life Coaching Goals

**This page will guide you in defining where you see yourself today in each life area.**

**Gauge and circle** the number that represents where you perceive yourself to be at the present time in each of the areas of your life. The range that you see yourself is from 0-Terrible to 10-Great.
Example: In the relationship area of your life, you might see yourself as needing to do better, so you would circle the number 2.

0    1    (2)    3    4    5    6    7    8    9    10

Terrible  Not So Good  Better  Average    Pretty good    Very good   Great

*All Relationships (Family-Friends-Dating)* **Scale 0-10**
0    1    2    3    4    5    6    7    8    9    10

*Health & Wellness* **Scale 0-10**
0    1    2    3    4    5    6    7    8    9    10

*Social Life & Fun* **Scale 0-10**
0    1    2    3    4    5    6    7    8    9    10

*School* S **Scale 0-10**
0    1    2    3    4    5    6    7    8    9    10

*Future Plans* **Scale 0-10**
0    1    2    3    4    5    6    7    8    9    10

*Spiritual* **Scale 0-10**
0    1    2    3    4    5    6    7    8    9    10

## Prioritize Each of the Areas 1 – 6

Number 1 is your most important area that you want to address first and number 6 is your least important area to work on.

(EX. If your most important area is School… place a 1 on School)

Relationships___ Health & Wellness___ Social/Fun___
School___ Future Plans___ Spiritual___

There is a section for each life area and you will start by going to the section that you identified as your number one highest priority. (Example: If your # 1 priority that you want to start working on first is school, then go to the school section and complete it.

You will then move on to the section of your number two priority that you listed.

As you complete the journaling exercises in one section, and then go to the next highest priority section you will continue on until each of the six sections is completed.

# Effective Goal Setting

*"The greater danger for most of us lies not in setting our aim too high and falling short; but in setting our aim too low, and achieving our mark."*
– Michelangelo Buonarrot

We are going to move onto goal setting. Goals are something that you want to be, to have or to do. In the 6 areas of life you will start by writing down as many goals as can think of in one particular area.

You will determine which is your one major goal and then include up to three additional goals if you have that many.

Make sure your goals are specific and ones that you realistically can attain. (Examples: To lose 10 pounds. To become a writer. To communicate better with my mom. To have positive friends).

Express your goals positively.

Once you identify your goals, you will explore possible action steps to make reaching your goals possible. (Examples: I will eat healthy food. I will use a tutor. I will join a church youth group. I will work out at the gym 2 times a week).

# Life Coaching

Open journal about whatever is in your heart today.
Remember to include the positive!

_____

_____

_____

_____

_____

_____

_____

_____

_____

_____

_____

_____

_____

_____

_____

_____

_____

_____

_____

_____

_____

_____

_____

_____

_____

_____

_____

_____

_____

_____

_____

_____

*Relationship Goals*          **My Priority # _____**

## What goals or possibilities would you like to achieve in your relationships?

A goal is something that you want to be, to have or to do.
Write down as many goals as you really want to achieve in your relationship area. Ensure your goal is specific and realistic.
Express your goals positively. Ensure your goal is measurable.
(Examples: To make one new positive friend. To improve communication with my mother).

Goals:_____

_____

_____

_____

_____

_____

_____

What will achieving your goals mean to you?  What would it look ...feel...sound like?

_____

_____

_____

_____

_____

What specific action steps would you commit to and work hard for, in order to achieve your relationship goal(s)?

_____

_____

_____

_____

_____

_____

_____

_____

What roadblocks/fears have prevented you from achieving your relationship(s) goal(s)?

_____

_____

_____

_____

What specific actions can you take to work around each roadblock?

_____

_____

_____

_____

What actions can you take to let go of your fears in order to stop worrying about what might happen.

_____

_____

_____

_____

Describe your skills or other resources that are available to you that would help you to achieve your relationship goals.

_____

_____

_____

_____

What other resources do you need?

_____

_____

_____

_____

Describe a plan that you can adopt in order to keep yourself on track and accountable for your progress in reaching this goal(s).

_____

_____

_____

_____

_____

# Life Coaching

Open journal about whatever is in your heart today.
Remember to include the positive!

_____

_____

_____

_____

_____

_____

_____

_____

_____

_____

_____

_____

_____

_____

_____

_____

_____

_____

_____

_____

_____

_____

_____

_____

_____

_____

_____

_____

_____

_____

_____

_____

# *Relationship Goal* Visualization & Written Affirmation

Use your worksheets to make an affirmation statement using the words you used to answer the questions. (Example below). Journal your affirmation statement and on a daily basis, take a few minutes of quiet time and re- read your goal affirmation.

## My Relationship Positive Goal Affirmation

_____

_____

_____

_____

_____

_____

_____

_____

_____

_____

_____

_____

_____

_____

_____

_____

_____

### Affirmation EXAMPLE

I am so thankful that I have exceeded my expectations for deepening my current relationship with my mother and for acquiring 3 new positive friends. I am so easy to talk to and I now am open and confident in my relationships. I easily share my deepest heart-thoughts with others. I am happy and loved as I relax around others. I am now free and open... I communicate openly and honestly.

### Visualization

Close your eyes and look through the picture window and visualize a compelling vision of you in the future and imagine yourself as if you have already achieved your relationship goals. The more you visualize your goals as being true now, and as you start acting the way you envision yourself, the more you will feel empowered and whole.

# Life Coaching

Open journal about whatever is in your heart today.
Remember to include the positive!

_____

_____

_____

_____

_____

_____

_____

_____

_____

_____

_____

_____

_____

_____

_____

_____

_____

_____

_____

_____

_____

_____

_____

_____

_____

_____

_____

_____

_____

_____

_____

_____

_____

*Health & Wellness*                    *Priority___*

**What goals or possibilities would you like to achieve in Health & Wellness?**
A goal is something that you want to be, to have or to do.
Write down as many goals as you really want to achieve in that area.
Ensure your goal is specific and realistic: (To run a marathon. To lose 10 pounds.) Express your goals positively.

Goals:_____

_____

_____

_____

_____

_____

What will achieving your goals mean to you?  What would it look …feel… sound like?

_____

_____

_____

_____

What specific action steps would you commit to and work hard for, in order to achieve your Health & Wellness goal(s)?

_____

_____

_____

_____

What roadblocks/fears have prevented you from achieving your Health & Wellness(s) goal(s)?

_____

_____

_____

What specific actions can you take to work around each roadblock?

_____
_____
_____
_____

What actions can you take to let go of your fears in order to stop worrying about what might happen.

_____
_____
_____
_____

Describe your skills or other resources that are available to you that would help you to achieve your Health & Wellness goals.

_____
_____
_____
_____

What other resources do you need?

_____
_____
_____
_____

Describe a plan that you can adopt in order to keep yourself on track and accountable for your progress in reaching this goal(s).

_____
_____
_____
_____
_____
_____
_____
_____
_____
_____

## Life Coaching

Open journal about whatever is in your heart today.
Remember to include the positive!

_____
_____
_____
_____
_____
_____
_____
_____
_____
_____
_____
_____
_____
_____
_____
_____
_____
_____
_____
_____
_____
_____
_____
_____
_____
_____
_____
_____
_____

## *Health & Wellness Goal Visualization & Written Affirmation*

Use your worksheets to make an affirmation statement using the words you used to answer the questions. Journal your affirmation statement and on a daily basis, take a few minutes of quiet time and re- read your goal affirmation.

### My Health & Wellness Positive Goal Affirmation

_____
_____
_____
_____
_____
_____
_____
_____
_____
_____
_____
_____
_____
_____
_____

### Affirmation EXAMPLE

Now that I eat healthy and exercise... more wellness activities now come so easy and natural. I am so proud knowing that I have added years to my life. I'm so fit now that I exercise on a regular basis and I feel more secure about my health... I now find it natural and easy to live healthy. I have higher energy as I now eat healthier foods and exercise... in fact, I am so active with the kids that now it's easy to say yes when they ask me to ride with them on rides... including the roller coaster. I comfortably participate in so many other fun activities with friends and family.

### Visualization EXAMPLE

Close your eyes and look through the picture window and visualize a compelling vision of you in a setting in the future and imagine yourself as if you have already achieved your Health & Wellness goals. The more you visualize your goals as current realities, and as you start acting the way you envision yourself, the more you will feel empowered and whole.

## Life Coaching

Open journal about whatever is in your heart today.
Remember to include the positive!

### *School Goals*                    *Priority* ____

**What School goals or possibilities would you like to achieve?**

A goal is something that you want to be, to have or to do.
Write down as many goals as you really want to achieve in that area.
Ensure your goal is specific and realistic: (To raise my math grade. To graduate.)
Express your goals positively. Ensure your goal is measurable. (I want to get at least a C in math. I want to get all Cs or higher on my report card).

Goals:_____
_____
_____
_____
_____
_____
_____
_____
_____
_____

What will achieving your goals mean to you?  What would it look ...feel...sound like?
_____
_____
_____
_____

What specific action steps would you commit to and work hard for, in order to achieve your School goal(s)?
_____
_____
_____
_____

What roadblocks/fears have prevented you from achieving your School goal(s)?

_____

_____

_____

_____

What specific actions can you take to work around each roadblock?

_____

_____

_____

_____

What actions can you take to let go of your fears in order to stop worrying about what might happen.

_____

_____

_____

_____

Describe your skills or other resources that are available to you that would help you to achieve your School goals.

_____

_____

_____

What other resources do you need?

_____

_____

_____

Describe a plan that you can adopt in order to keep yourself on track and accountable for your progress in reaching this goal(s).

_____

_____

_____

_____

_____

_____

# Life Coaching

Open journal about whatever is in your heart today.
Remember to include the positive!

## *School Goal* Visualization & Written Affirmation

Use your worksheets to make a School affirmation statement using the words you used to answer the questions. Journal your affirmation statement and on a daily basis, take a few minutes of quiet time and re- read your goal affirmation.

### My Professional Positive Goal Affirmation

_____
_____
_____
_____
_____
_____
_____
_____
_____
_____
_____
_____
_____
_____
_____
_____

### Affirmation EXAMPLE

I have achieved confidence and inner peace now that I do my homework at a certain time each day. I am thrilled that I now earn grades higher than Cs on each report card. I have enhanced my educational confidence and I am concentrating on finding a college that I want to attend after graduation.

### Visualization EXAMPLE

Close your eyes and look through the picture window and visualize a compelling vision of you in a setting in the future and imagine yourself as if you have already achieved your School goals. The more you visualize your goals as current realities, and as you start acting the way you envision yourself, the more you will feel empowered and whole.

# Life Coaching

Open journal about whatever is in your heart today.
Remember to include the positive!

## Social Life and Fun          Priority _____

**What goals or possibilities would you like to achieve?**
A goal is something that you want to be, to have or to do.
Write down as many goals as you really want to achieve in that area.
Ensure your goal is specific and realistic: To join a sister-hood group. To get my driver's license. Express your goals positively. Ensure it's measurable.

Goals:_____
_____
_____
_____
_____
_____
_____
_____
_____

What will achieving your goals mean to you?  What would it look
...feel...sound like?
_____
_____
_____
_____
_____
_____

What specific action steps would you commit to and work hard for, in order to achieve your Social goal(s)?
_____
_____
_____
_____
_____
_____

What roadblocks/fears have prevented you from achieving your Social goal(s)?

_____

_____

_____

_____

What specific actions can you take to work around each roadblock?

_____

_____

_____

_____

What actions can you take to let go of your fears in order to stop worrying about what might happen.

_____

_____

_____

_____

Describe your skills or other resources that are available to you that would help you to achieve your Social goals.

_____

_____

_____

_____

What other resources do you need?

_____

_____

_____

_____

Describe a plan that you can adopt in order to keep yourself on track and accountable for your progress in reaching this goal(s).

_____

_____

_____

_____

## Life Coaching

Open journal about whatever is in your heart today.
Remember to include the positive!

_____
_____
_____
_____
_____
_____
_____
_____
_____
_____
_____
_____
_____
_____
_____
_____
_____
_____
_____
_____
_____
_____
_____
_____
_____
_____
_____
_____
_____
_____
_____

*Social-Fun Goal Visualization & Written Affirmation*

Use your worksheets to make an affirmation statement using the words you used to answer the questions. Journal your affirmation statement and on a daily basis, take a few minutes of quiet time and re- read your goal affirmation.

### My Social-Fun Life Positive Goal Affirmation

_____
_____
_____
_____
_____
_____
_____
_____
_____
_____
_____
_____
_____
_____
_____
_____
_____
_____

### Affirmation EXAMPLE

I now have complete inner self-confidence in my decisions regarding my social life. With my support system and self-help activities... I have learned to say 'no' and that has helped me to achieve a more mature social life. I naturally and easily generate an abundance of positive inner and outer confidence in each aspect of my social life and I only participate in the activities that I truly think I will enjoy.

### Visualization EXAMPLE

Close your eyes and look through the picture window and visualize a compelling vision of you in a setting in the future and imagine yourself as if you have already achieved your Social-Fun goals. The more you visualize your goals as current realities, and as you start acting the way you envision yourself, the more you will feel empowered and whole.

147

# Life Coaching

Open journal about whatever is in your heart today.
Remember to include the positive!

*Future Plans Goals*                    *Priority* ___

## What goals or possibilities would you like to achieve in your Future Plans?

A goal is something that you want to be, to have or to do.
Write down as many goals as you really want to achieve in that area.
Ensure your goal is specific and realistic: To get a degree in Business. To own my own business. To be financially stable and to buy a home. Express your goals positively. Ensure your goal is measurable.

Goals:_____

_____

_____

_____

_____

_____

_____

_____


What will achieving your goals mean to you?  What would it look ...feel...sound like?

_____

_____

_____

_____


What specific action steps would you commit to and work hard for, in order to achieve your financial goal(s)?

_____

_____

_____

_____

_____

What roadblocks/fears have prevented you from planning your Future goal(s)?

_____

_____

_____

_____

_____

_____

What specific actions can you take to work around each roadblock?

_____

_____

_____

_____

What actions can you take to let go of your fears in order to stop worrying about what might happen.

_____

_____

_____

_____

Describe your skills or other resources that are available to you that would help you to achieve your Future goals.

_____

_____

_____

_____

What other resources do you need?

_____

_____

_____

_____

Describe a plan that you can adopt in order to keep yourself on track and accountable for your progress in reaching this goal(s).

_____

_____

_____

_____

_____

# Life Coaching

Open journal about whatever is in your heart today.
Remember to include the positive!

_____

_____

_____

_____

_____

_____

_____

_____

_____

_____

_____

_____

_____

_____

_____

_____

_____

_____

_____

_____

_____

_____

_____

_____

_____

_____

_____

_____

## *My Future Goal* Visualization & Written Affirmation

Use your worksheets to make an affirmation statement using the words you used to answer the questions. Journal your affirmation statement and on a daily basis, take a few minutes of quiet time and re- read your goal affirmation.

### My Future Life Positive Goal Affirmation

_____
_____
_____
_____
_____
_____
_____
_____
_____
_____
_____
_____
_____
_____
_____
_____
_____
_____

### Affirmation EXAMPLE

With my college degree in business, I now own a successful business that provides me an abundance that is sufficient to generously cover my family's living expenses. I generously donate to charity. I'm extremely excited for the opportunity I now have to travel around the world.

### Visualization EXAMPLE

Close your eyes and look through the picture window and visualize a compelling vision of you in a setting in the future and imagine yourself as if you have already achieved your Future goals. The more you visualize your goals as current realities, and as you start acting the way you envision yourself, the more you will feel empowered and whole.

# Life Coaching

Open journal about whatever is in your heart today.
Remember to include the positive!

## *Spiritual Goals*

### What goals or possibilities would you like to achieve in your Spiritual Life?

A goal is something that you want to be, to have or to do.
Write down as many goals as you really want to achieve in that area.
Ensure your goal is specific and realistic:
Express your goals positively.
Ensure your goal is measurable. To go on mission trips. To help others meet their needs.

Goals:_____
_____
_____
_____
_____
_____
_____
_____
_____

What will achieving your goals mean to you?  What would it look …feel…sound like?
_____
_____
_____
_____

What specific action steps would you commit to and work hard for, in order to achieve your spiritual goal(s)?
_____
_____
_____
_____
_____
_____

What roadblocks/fears would have prevented you from achieving your spiritual goal(s)?

_____

_____

_____

_____

What specific actions can you take to work around each roadblock?

_____

_____

_____

_____

What actions can you take to let go of your fears in order to stop worrying about what might happen.

_____

_____

_____

_____

Describe your skills or other resources that are available to you that would help you to achieve your spiritual goals.

_____

_____

_____

What other resources do you need?

_____

_____

_____

Describe a plan that you can adopt in order to keep yourself on track and accountable for your progress in reaching this goal(s).

_____

_____

_____

_____

_____

_____

## Life Coaching

Open journal about whatever is in your heart today.
Remember to include the positive!

# Life Coaching Prompt Topic:
## *Spiritual Goal Visualization & Written Affirmation*

Use your worksheets to make an affirmation statement using the words you used to answer the questions. Journal your affirmation statement and on a daily basis, take a few minutes of quiet time and re- read your goal affirmation.

### My Spiritual Life Positive Goal Affirmation

_____
_____
_____
_____
_____
_____
_____
_____
_____
_____
_____
_____
_____
_____
_____
_____
_____

### Affirmation EXAMPLE
I am excited that I now have true compassion and a heart of pure love for each person I meet. Even with my busy schedule ... I attend church and I never miss a day being inspired by music and meditations. I meet with my supportive circle of friends and as a group we are inspired by meditations, devotions and prayer. My vibrant faith balances and enhances all the aspects of my life.

### Visualization EXAMPLE
Close your eyes and look through the picture window and visualize a compelling vision of you in a setting in the future and imagine yourself as if you have already achieved your spiritual goals. The more you visualize your goals as current realities, and as you start acting the way you envision yourself, the more you will feel empowered and whole.

# Life Coaching

Open journal about whatever is in your heart today.
Remember to include the positive!

# Part II

As you work towards your goals, the second part of the journey will further supplement your inner growth as you move beyond.

Part II includes one to four inspirational words each day that will serve to inspire you as you continue to compose your life-song with your heart.

Over your lifetime, as you grow and change, this Life Coaching Journal can be used over and over by using notebooks to write your journaling responses.

You can dance anywhere, even if only in your heart. —Author Unknown

## Life Coaching Inspirational Words:  Mornings

Open journal about whatever is in your heart today.
Remember to include the positive!

_____
_____
_____
_____
_____
_____
_____
_____
_____
_____
_____
_____
_____
_____
_____
_____
_____
_____
_____
_____
_____
_____
_____
_____
_____
_____
_____
_____
_____

# Life Coaching Inspirational Words:  Today I Will…
Open journal about whatever is in your heart today.
Remember to include the positive!

## Life Coaching Inspirational Words:  I am so.....

Open journal about whatever is in your heart today.
Remember to include the positive!

_____
_____
_____
_____
_____
_____
_____
_____
_____
_____
_____
_____
_____
_____
_____
_____
_____
_____
_____
_____
_____
_____
_____
_____
_____
_____
_____
_____
_____
_____
_____

# Life Coaching Inspirational Words: Overlook

Open journal about whatever is in your heart today.
Remember to include the positive!

_____

_____

_____

_____

_____

_____

_____

_____

_____

_____

_____

_____

_____

_____

_____

_____

_____

_____

_____

_____

_____

_____

_____

_____

_____

_____

_____

_____

_____

## Life Coaching Inspirational Words:  Peter Pan

Open journal about whatever is in your heart today.
Remember to include the positive!

_____
_____
_____
_____
_____
_____
_____
_____
_____
_____
_____
_____
_____
_____
_____
_____
_____
_____
_____
_____
_____
_____
_____
_____
_____
_____
_____
_____
_____
_____

# Life Coaching Inspirational Words:  My Dream

Open journal about whatever is in your heart today.
Remember to include the positive!

_____
_____
_____
_____
_____
_____
_____
_____
_____
_____
_____
_____
_____
_____
_____
_____
_____
_____
_____
_____
_____
_____
_____
_____
_____
_____
_____
_____
_____
_____
_____
_____
_____

# Life Coaching Inspirational Words:  Forever

Open journal about whatever is in your heart today.
Remember to include the positive!

# Life Coaching Inspirational Words: Seasons
Open journal about whatever is in your heart today.
Remember to include the positive!

_____
_____
_____
_____
_____
_____
_____
_____
_____
_____
_____
_____
_____
_____
_____
_____
_____
_____
_____
_____
_____
_____
_____
_____
_____
_____
_____
_____
_____
_____
_____
_____

## Life Coaching Inspirational Words: An old friend

Open journal about whatever is in your heart today.
Remember to include the positive!

_____

_____

_____

_____

_____

_____

_____

_____

_____

_____

_____

_____

_____

_____

_____

_____

_____

_____

_____

_____

_____

_____

_____

_____

_____

_____

_____

_____

_____

_____

_____

_____

_____

_____

## Life Coaching Inspirational Words:   A new friend
Open journal about whatever is in your heart today.
Remember to include the positive!

# Life Coaching Inspirational Words: Genuine

Open journal about whatever is in your heart today.
Remember to include the positive!

_____
_____
_____
_____
_____
_____
_____
_____
_____
_____
_____
_____
_____
_____
_____
_____
_____
_____
_____
_____
_____
_____
_____
_____
_____
_____
_____
_____
_____
_____
_____

## Life Coaching:        TV show

Open journal about whatever is in your heart today.
Remember to include the positive!

_____
_____
_____
_____
_____
_____
_____
_____
_____
_____
_____
_____
_____
_____
_____
_____
_____
_____
_____
_____
_____
_____
_____
_____
_____
_____
_____
_____
_____
_____

## Life Coaching: Video game

Open journal about whatever is in your heart today.
Remember to include the positive!

_____
_____
_____
_____
_____
_____
_____
_____
_____
_____
_____
_____
_____
_____
_____
_____
_____
_____
_____
_____
_____
_____
_____
_____
_____
_____
_____
_____
_____
_____
_____
_____

## Life Coaching:        Movie

Open journal about whatever is in your heart today.
Remember to include the positive!

_____
_____
_____
_____
_____
_____
_____
_____
_____
_____
_____
_____
_____
_____
_____
_____
_____
_____
_____
_____
_____
_____
_____
_____
_____
_____
_____
_____
_____
_____
_____

## Life Coaching:    Beliefs

Open journal about whatever is in your heart today.
Remember to include the positive!

_____
_____
_____
_____
_____
_____
_____
_____
_____
_____
_____
_____
_____
_____
_____
_____
_____
_____
_____
_____
_____
_____
_____
_____
_____
_____
_____
_____

## Life Coaching:        Expectations

Open journal about whatever is in your heart today.
Remember to include the positive!

**Life Coaching:**     **Grateful for…**

Open journal about whatever is in your heart today.
Remember to include the positive!

## Life Coaching:  I deserve...

Open journal about whatever is in your heart today.
Remember to include the positive!

_____
_____
_____
_____
_____
_____
_____
_____
_____
_____
_____
_____
_____
_____
_____
_____
_____
_____
_____
_____
_____
_____
_____
_____
_____
_____
_____
_____
_____
_____

## Life Coaching:    My inner wisdom...

Open journal about whatever is in your heart today.
Remember to include the positive!

_____

_____

_____

_____

_____

_____

_____

_____

_____

_____

_____

_____

_____

_____

_____

_____

_____

_____

_____

_____

_____

_____

_____

_____

_____

_____

_____

_____

_____

_____

_____

_____

## Life Coaching:    Strong girls...

Open journal about whatever is in your heart today.
Remember to include the positive!

## Life Coaching:        More of who I am....

Open journal about whatever is in your heart today.
Remember to include the positive!

_____
_____
_____
_____
_____
_____
_____
_____
_____
_____
_____
_____
_____
_____
_____
_____
_____
_____
_____
_____
_____
_____
_____
_____
_____
_____
_____
_____
_____
_____
_____
_____

## Life Coaching:      Growing & changing….

Open journal about whatever is in your heart today.
Remember to include the positive!

## Life Coaching:    I claim my ability to change...

Open journal about whatever is in your heart today.
Remember to include the positive!

_____
_____
_____
_____
_____
_____
_____
_____
_____
_____
_____
_____
_____
_____
_____
_____
_____
_____
_____
_____
_____
_____
_____
_____
_____
_____
_____
_____
_____
_____
_____

## Life Coaching:          This week I will…..

Open journal about whatever is in your heart today.
Remember to include the positive!

_____

_____

_____

_____

_____

_____

_____

_____

_____

_____

_____

_____

_____

_____

_____

_____

_____

_____

_____

_____

_____

_____

_____

_____

_____

_____

_____

_____

## Life Coaching:     Accepting those who are different

Open journal about whatever is in your heart today.
Remember to include the positive!

_____

_____

_____

_____

_____

_____

_____

_____

_____

_____

_____

_____

_____

_____

_____

_____

_____

_____

_____

_____

_____

_____

_____

_____

_____

_____

_____

_____

_____

_____

_____

## Life Coaching:  Love people

Open journal about whatever is in your heart today.
Remember to include the positive!

_____

_____

_____

_____

_____

_____

_____

_____

_____

_____

_____

_____

_____

_____

_____

_____

_____

_____

_____

_____

_____

_____

_____

_____

_____

_____

_____

_____

_____

_____

## Life Coaching:      Rainbows

Open journal about whatever is in your heart today.
Remember to include the positive!

_____

_____

_____

_____

_____

_____

_____

_____

_____

_____

_____

_____

_____

_____

_____

_____

_____

_____

_____

_____

_____

_____

_____

_____

_____

_____

_____

_____

_____

## Life Coaching:     There's a solution

Open journal about whatever is in your heart today.
Remember to include the positive!

## Life Coaching:     Home

Open journal about whatever is in your heart today.
Remember to include the positive!

_____

_____

_____

_____

_____

_____

_____

_____

_____

_____

_____

_____

_____

_____

_____

_____

_____

_____

_____

_____

_____

_____

_____

_____

_____

_____

_____

_____

## Life Coaching:     Power to change

Open journal about whatever is in your heart today.
Remember to include the positive!

_____

_____

_____

_____

_____

_____

_____

_____

_____

_____

_____

_____

_____

_____

_____

_____

_____

_____

_____

_____

_____

_____

_____

_____

_____

_____

_____

_____

_____

_____

_____

_____

_____

_____

## Life Coaching:      My heart

Open journal about whatever is in your heart today.
Remember to include the positive!

_____

_____

_____

_____

_____

_____

_____

_____

_____

_____

_____

_____

_____

_____

_____

_____

_____

_____

_____

_____

_____

_____

_____

_____

_____

_____

_____

_____

_____

_____

_____

_____

## Life Coaching:          My journey

Open journal about whatever is in your heart today.
Remember to include the positive!

**Life Coaching:**         **Singing my song**

Open journal about whatever is in your heart today.
Remember to include the positive!

_____
_____
_____
_____
_____
_____
_____
_____
_____
_____
_____
_____
_____
_____
_____
_____
_____
_____
_____
_____
_____
_____
_____
_____
_____
_____
_____
_____
_____
_____

## Life Coaching:      Loving my....

Open journal about whatever is in your heart today.
Remember to include the positive!

## Life Coaching:        Inspiring...

Open journal about whatever is in your heart today.
Remember to include the positive!

## Life Coaching:          Healing….

Open journal about whatever is in your heart today.
Remember to include the positive!

## Life Coaching:          Composer of .....

Open journal about whatever is in your heart today.
Remember to include the positive!

_____

_____

_____

_____

_____

_____

_____

_____

_____

_____

_____

_____

_____

_____

_____

_____

_____

_____

_____

_____

_____

_____

_____

## Life Coaching:     Conductor of…..

Open journal about whatever is in your heart today.
Remember to include the positive!

_____
_____
_____
_____
_____
_____
_____
_____
_____
_____
_____
_____
_____
_____
_____
_____
_____
_____
_____
_____
_____
_____
_____
_____
_____
_____
_____
_____
_____
_____
_____
_____

## Life Coaching:     Director of ....

Open journal about whatever is in your heart today.
Remember to include the positive!

_____

_____

_____

_____

_____

_____

_____

_____

_____

_____

_____

_____

_____

_____

_____

_____

_____

_____

_____

_____

_____

_____

_____

_____

_____

_____

_____

_____

_____

_____

## Life Coaching: I live life

Open journal about whatever is in your heart today.
Remember to include the positive!

_____
_____
_____
_____
_____
_____
_____
_____
_____
_____
_____
_____
_____
_____
_____
_____
_____
_____
_____
_____
_____
_____
_____
_____
_____
_____
_____
_____
_____
_____
_____
_____

## Life Coaching:          Choice =

Open journal about whatever is in your heart today.
Remember to include the positive!

_____

_____

_____

_____

_____

_____

_____

_____

_____

_____

_____

_____

_____

_____

_____

_____

_____

_____

_____

_____

_____

_____

_____

_____

_____

_____

_____

_____

## Life Coaching:     Personal power

Open journal about whatever is in your heart today.
Remember to include the positive!

## Life Coaching: _____ rocks!!

Open journal about whatever is in your heart today.
Remember to include the positive!

_____

_____

_____

_____

_____

_____

_____

_____

_____

_____

_____

_____

_____

_____

_____

_____

_____

_____

_____

_____

_____

_____

_____

_____

_____

_____

_____

_____

_____

_____

_____

_____

## Life Coaching:     It leads to …..

Open journal about whatever is in your heart today.
Remember to include the positive!

## Life Coaching:     **Black & blue**

Open journal about whatever is in your heart today.
Remember to include the positive!

_____
_____
_____
_____
_____
_____
_____
_____
_____
_____
_____
_____
_____
_____
_____
_____
_____
_____
_____
_____
_____
_____
_____
_____
_____
_____
_____
_____
_____
_____

## Life Coaching:        Happiness

Open journal about whatever is in your heart today.
Remember to include the positive!

_____

_____

_____

_____

_____

_____

_____

_____

_____

_____

_____

_____

_____

_____

_____

_____

_____

_____

_____

_____

_____

_____

_____

_____

_____

_____

_____

_____

_____

## Life Coaching:  Comforting

Open journal about whatever is in your heart today.
Remember to include the positive!

_____

_____

_____

_____

_____

_____

_____

_____

_____

_____

_____

_____

_____

_____

_____

_____

_____

_____

_____

_____

_____

_____

_____

_____

_____

_____

_____

_____

_____

## Life Coaching:          Good times

Open journal about whatever is in your heart today.
Remember to include the positive!

_____
_____
_____
_____
_____
_____
_____
_____
_____
_____
_____
_____
_____
_____
_____
_____
_____
_____
_____
_____
_____
_____
_____
_____
_____
_____
_____
_____
_____
_____
_____
_____

## Life Coaching:     Clouds

Open journal about whatever is in your heart today.
Remember to include the positive!

_____
_____
_____
_____
_____
_____
_____
_____
_____
_____
_____
_____
_____
_____
_____
_____
_____
_____
_____
_____
_____
_____
_____
_____
_____
_____
_____
_____
_____
_____
_____

## Life Coaching:        Creating

Open journal about whatever is in your heart today.
Remember to include the positive!

_____

_____

_____

_____

_____

_____

_____

_____

_____

_____

_____

_____

_____

_____

_____

_____

_____

_____

_____

_____

_____

_____

_____

_____

_____

_____

_____

## Life Coaching:     Living life

Open journal about whatever is in your heart today.
Remember to include the positive!

_____
_____
_____
_____
_____
_____
_____
_____
_____
_____
_____
_____
_____
_____
_____
_____
_____
_____
_____
_____
_____
_____
_____
_____
_____
_____
_____
_____
_____

## Life Coaching:　　　　My heart sings

Open journal about whatever is in your heart today.
Remember to include the positive!

_____

_____

_____

_____

_____

_____

_____

_____

_____

_____

_____

_____

_____

_____

_____

_____

_____

_____

_____

_____

_____

_____

_____

_____

_____

_____

_____

_____

_____

_____

_____

_____

## Life Coaching:          The game changer

Open journal about whatever is in your heart today.
Remember to include the positive!

_____

_____

_____

_____

_____

_____

_____

_____

_____

_____

_____

_____

_____

_____

_____

_____

_____

_____

_____

_____

_____

_____

_____

_____

_____

_____

_____

_____

_____

_____

## Life Coaching:          What?

Open journal about whatever is in your heart today.
Remember to include the positive!

_____

_____

_____

_____

_____

_____

_____

_____

_____

_____

_____

_____

_____

_____

_____

_____

_____

_____

_____

_____

_____

_____

_____

_____

_____

_____

_____

_____

## Life Coaching:          Blue skies

Open journal about whatever is in your heart today.
Remember to include the positive!

_____
_____
_____
_____
_____
_____
_____
_____
_____
_____
_____
_____
_____
_____
_____
_____
_____
_____
_____
_____
_____
_____
_____
_____
_____
_____
_____
_____
_____
_____
_____

## Life Coaching:     Under construction

Open journal about whatever is in your heart today.
Remember to include the positive!

_____

_____

_____

_____

_____

_____

_____

_____

_____

_____

_____

_____

_____

_____

_____

_____

_____

_____

_____

_____

_____

_____

_____

_____

_____

_____

_____

_____

_____

_____

_____

## Life Coaching:          Courage to …..

Open journal about whatever is in your heart today.
Remember to include the positive!

## Life Coaching:        SMILE

Open journal about whatever is in your heart today.
Remember to include the positive!

_____

_____

_____

_____

_____

_____

_____

_____

_____

_____

_____

_____

_____

_____

_____

_____

_____

_____

_____

_____

_____

_____

_____

_____

_____

_____

_____

_____

_____

_____

_____

_____

_____

## Life Coaching:  Bloom where I'm planted

Open journal about whatever is in your heart today.
Remember to include the positive!

_____

_____

_____

_____

_____

_____

_____

_____

_____

_____

_____

_____

_____

_____

_____

_____

_____

_____

_____

_____

_____

_____

_____

_____

_____

_____

_____

_____

_____

_____

_____

_____

_____

## Life Coaching: Change changes.......

Open journal about whatever is in your heart today.
Remember to include the positive!

## Life Coaching:          My parents…..

Open journal about whatever is in your heart today.
Remember to include the positive!

_____

_____

_____

_____

_____

_____

_____

_____

_____

_____

_____

_____

_____

_____

_____

_____

_____

_____

_____

_____

_____

_____

_____

_____

_____

_____

_____

_____

_____

_____

## Life Coaching:     I've cried myself......

Open journal about whatever is in your heart today.
Remember to include the positive!

_____

_____

_____

_____

_____

_____

_____

_____

_____

_____

_____

_____

_____

_____

_____

_____

_____

_____

_____

_____

_____

_____

_____

_____

_____

_____

_____

_____

_____

_____

_____

**Life Coaching:**          **Love to play….**

Open journal about whatever is in your heart today.
Remember to include the positive!

_____

_____

_____

_____

_____

_____

_____

_____

_____

_____

_____

_____

_____

_____

_____

_____

_____

_____

_____

_____

_____

_____

_____

_____

_____

_____

_____

_____

_____

_____

_____

_____

## Life Coaching:     No umbrellas needed

Open journal about whatever is in your heart today.
Remember to include the positive!

_____

_____

_____

_____

_____

_____

_____

_____

_____

_____

_____

_____

_____

_____

_____

_____

_____

_____

_____

_____

_____

_____

_____

_____

_____

_____

_____

_____

_____

_____

_____

_____

## Life Coaching:          Self-discipline

Open journal about whatever is in your heart today.
Remember to include the positive!